Contemporary Monologues for Young Actors
2

Douglas M. Parker

ISBN-13: 978-1-7340014-0-2
ISBN-10: 1-7340014-0-2

For my own contemporaries,
Sam, Michael and Tom

Also by Douglas M. Parker

Contemporary Monologues for Young Actors

Fantasy Monologues for Young Actors

Contemporary Scenes for Young Actors

CONTENTS

INTRODUCTION

A monologue is a very special kind of performance. One that takes place between a single actor and an audience, often without sets, props, costumes or lighting. It is theater slimmed down to its very essence.

This means that every time a monologue is presented – whether as a performance piece, an audition piece, or an acting exercise – it's an opportunity for young actors to build an unusually direct connection with the audience. To reveal and develop strengths they never knew they had. And to generate a unique kind of magic.

With that thought in mind, the 54 monologues contained in this book provide younger actors with the opportunity to explore a full range of age-appropriate characters, emotions and situations. Of equal importance, the language used in each monologue is typical everyday language, allowing younger performers to focus directly on each piece, without being distracted by unfamiliar words or turns of phrase.

Who Is This Book For?

For the most part, the monologues in this book were created for actors and acting students aged 7-14, as well as for the teachers, directors and acting coaches who work with them. As you look over the possibilities, you'll notice that some of the selections may work better for actors toward the lower end of that age range, while others may work better for actors toward the upper end. Simply choose for yourself or your students the pieces that seem to be the best fit, and that offer the best learning, acting or audition possibilities.

Although there is no particular order to the monologues presented, some of the monologues toward the beginning of the book may work better for slightly younger actors, while some of the later monologues may work better for slightly older actors.

A Quick Word for Actors

Every monologue was created to work equally well for male and female actors, which means that any monologue in this book could be right for you. Simply choose whichever pieces appeal to you the most, or that allow you to explore particular emotions, situations or acting challenges.

Once you've chosen a monologue, if it makes you feel more comfortable with the material to change a word or a name, go ahead and do it. Similarly, although some minimal stage directions are given above or within many of the monologues, feel free to follow or ignore any suggestions made. This is your performance, bring it to life in your own way.

Finally, before you present any of the pieces, remember to ask yourself what the character you've chosen is really thinking, really feeling, and really saying. Do your character's emotions or thinking change during the course of the monologue? And if so, when and why – and how can you best show that change? In the end, the more thought you put into your performance, the more enjoyment the audience will get out of your performance.

MONOLOGUES

MONOLOGUES

WARM UP

(Your character is standing outside in winter and is very, very cold.)

(Hugging yourself and shivering.)
Cold. Really cold. Ice cube, freezer, North Pole cold . . . Ugh – I can't even feel my toes anymore. I don't think I can deal with this. What did they say to do? Think warm thoughts.
(Close eyes and think.)
Warm thoughts . . . Summer. Beaches. Camp fires. Hot showers.
(Open eyes and look around. Thoughtfully.)
Huh.
(Close eyes again. Louder and more passionately.)
Steam rooms. Furnaces. Volcanoes. The middle of the sun!
(Open eyes, relax, and stop hugging yourself.)
Wow. Well . . .
(Pause a moment, looking relaxed.)
That didn't work at all.
(Instantly look cold again and start hugging yourself.)
Good to know.
(Walk off stiffly, still freezing.)

SECRETS

You know the best thing about secrets? Everything. I'm serious. First you get to feel special because you know something that no one else knows. And then you get to feel special all over again when you tell everyone this awesome secret that no one else knows! And yeah – I get that once you tell everyone something, it's not a secret anymore. But that's really kind of the point, isn't it? I mean, if you actually wanted to keep something secret, everyone knows I should be the *last* person you'd tell. Right? So yeah, anyone got any secrets they want to share? . . . Anyone?

HEROES

(Throughout the monologue, your character is having a possibly imaginary conversation with a real dog. Be sure to pause for the dog's responses, noted by three dots.)

(Crouch down and pet the dog once or twice as you speak.)

Good dog! Who's a good dog!

(Pause a moment and listen as the dog speaks.)

What's that, girl? . . . What!?! Angela fell down a well? . . . And she can't get out? All right, I need you to go to the North Centerville volunteer fire department and . . . No, the *North* Centerville volunteer fire department and ask for. . . Yes, North Centerville. And ask for the Fire Chief. Then tell him exactly what you told me – that Angela has fallen down a well and can't get out. Go on girl! Angela's in trouble!

(Listen intently as the dog speaks.)

Well, yes, I guess we could just hang out here instead . . . What's that, girl? You'd rather . . . What? . . . You'd rather sit on the sofa and watch TV with me? . . . And you also want us to both eat ice cream? . . . Chocolate chip ice cream with Reese's Pieces on top? OK, well it's up to you. You're the hero in the family. Let's go watch TV! Good girl! Good girl!

(Stand up. Glance back down at dog, then walk off, as dog follows you.)

QUESTION

I like to ask questions. About everything. Like – why does flammable mean the same thing as inflammable? Or, why don't different colors have different smells? Or, why doesn't Riley like me? I mean, he/she really should. I'm smart. I'm funny. I let him/her cheat off my math test. OK, so maybe we both failed that test. Like, embarrassingly. Like the two worst scores in the entire class . . . By far. But that doesn't mean that it wasn't a really nice thing for me to do. I mean, if Riley let *me* cheat off *his/her* test, I would totally get that he/she was telling me that he/she really likes me. Why are people so clueless? . . . And why can't you tickle yourself? And why do you wear less clothes to go in the shower, but more clothes to go in the rain? . . . Still, I guess if I could only know the answer to ten questions, it would be the ten questions that were on that math test. 'Cuz then Riley would like me now. At least, I think he/she would. I better ask someone.

GO FISH

(Your character is in the bathroom, standing next to the toilet. If you like, a chair can be used to represent the toilet. Stand solemnly for a moment before you speak. One of your hands is closed and holding something.)

Dearly beloved, we are gathered in this bathroom today not to mourn the death, but to celebrate the life, of Fluffy the goldfish.
(Lift your closed hand, which holds Fluffy's imaginary body. Open your hand and look down fondly at Fluffy.)
Those of you who have been to my room will remember the joy with which he swam around, and around, and around . . . and around his bowl. Endlessly. Or so we thought. Always curious, kind and brave – except when the cat was around – Fluffy had too many wonderful qualities to name here today. But whenever I think of Fluffy, the one thing I'll always remember is his sense of determination. How all day long he would circle, and circle, and circle . . . and circle his bowl, pushing ever onward. Some fish lack a sense of purpose. Some fish are quitters. Fluffy was not such a fish. So I believe – as we stand here in this bathroom today by Fluffy's final resting place – we can all take comfort in the thought that Fluffy's spirit will never truly leave us, and that he will simply go from circling one bowl to circling another.
(Lift the lid of the toilet seat and drop Fluffy's body into the toilet.)
And now, if no one has anything else to add, I'm going to say good-bye and flush the toilet.
(Flush toilet. Watch a moment as Fluffy's body circles and disappears, making small circling motions with your head as you watch. After a moment, look up at the ceiling.)
Good-bye, Fluffy.

INFINITE

(Throughout the monologue, you're holding a small, wrapped present behind your back, which can't be seen by the audience. The present can be real or imaginary.)

Last week, Mr. Cassidy in math was telling us about how there's infinity and then there are *magnitudes* of infinity. Like how, for instance, infinity is an amount of something that just goes on forever and ever and never ends. But then after that there are *magnitudes* of infinity. Like infinities that are even bigger than regular infinity. And other infinities that are even bigger than that. And I was thinking – yes, an infinity of infinities! That's exactly right. That's exactly how much I love you.

> *(Pull out the present from behind your back and hold it out.)*

Happy birthday, Mommy!

BITE

(Just before the monologue begins, start nervously biting your nails for a few moments.)

Yeah, I bite my nails. So what? Some people crack their knuckles. Some people play with their hair until it practically drives you crazy. And some people bite their nails. It doesn't mean I'm a nervous person if that's what you're thinking . . . That's what you were thinking, right? Yeah. Well, it doesn't. More like the opposite. I bite my nails to make myself *stop* being nervous. So if you see me biting my nails, that means I'm relaxed. Really relaxed. Super relaxed. So you don't need to think about it any more. About them. About me. I mean my nails. You can just think about something else. And I'll just be here relaxing . . . Really relaxed . . . Super relaxed.
(Look at the nails you've been biting.)
Yeah.

ENCOURAGEMENT

OK now, as the team captain and best player on the team, I just want to get everyone totally stoked before we start the game. Kelly, I just want to say that you did a great job against the Pencilville Porcupines last week. For like the first eight minutes – and then, well . . . anyway, good job! Taylor, I'm so proud of you. You have improved so much since the beginning of the season. I think that with a lot of work, one day you could be almost average. Casey, just remember that your job is not to follow the mascot around, it's to follow the ball. Do that and I'm pretty sure that you could be, um . . . useful. Everyone else, just try your hardest and maybe that will work. So let's go out there and have a great game. I really believe that just this once, with the right attitude, we might even make it to halftime. Go Turtles!

THE RIDE

Yesterday I was riding the bus. And it was hot and noisy and crowded, and I was not having a good time at all. But then I looked around and I started thinking about how everyone on the bus was totally different from each other. I mean, not just like different clothes and different hair and different looking, but with totally different lives and pasts and futures. But here, for just a little while, we were all together and going to the same place. And that's when it hit me that the bus was kind of like - I don't know - life I guess. I mean, everyone's got a different story, with a different beginning and a different ending, but for just a little while we're all here together. And so I just sort of wiggled down in my seat and I thought, maybe it *is* hot and maybe it *is* noisy and maybe it *is* crowded, but we're here now, so let's just enjoy the ride.

BURN

Ow. Ow, ow, ow. Ow. Yesterday me and Jordan hung out in the backyard trying to get the perfect tan. It didn't turn out perfect. I mean, how is it fair that you don't know you're sunburned until it's too late? You see this little part here?

(Touch your shoulder.)

Ow. It hurts when I touch it. You see this other little part over here?

(Touch a different part of yourself.)

Ow. It hurts even more when I touch it. And this part?

(Put your finger close to another part of yourself.)

It hurts even when I don't touch it.

(Touch it.)

Ow! But, honestly, name one other thing you can do that makes you look better than you already look and you don't have to do *anything*. I'm serious. You can actually check your phone or eat chocolate or *fall asleep* while getting a tan. And when you wake up, you look amazing. Does it hurt? Yeah. But is it worth it? So yeah. I mean, just look at me. 'Nuff said.

CALLING

After he moved out, my dad used to call every day. But after a while, it was more like a couple of times a week. Then maybe once a week. And now maybe a couple of times a month. But when he does call, we talk and talk. It's just so good hearing his voice. And I can kind of almost close my eyes and imagine that he's there, sitting across from me. And maybe we're about to play some game, or maybe go for a walk. Or just sit there and keep talking. But of course, sooner or later we have to get off the phone. He always says to me, you know, even though I'm not there I'm still a part of your life and you can tell me anything you want. But I can't. Not really. Because I can't say the only thing I really want to tell him. Come home. Just come home.

BEDTIME

(Your character is saying a bedtime prayer.)

(Kneel, put your hands together, and look up.)

Hi. It's me again. First, I want to thank you for the weather today. I mean, I know there's weather every day, but today it felt like you really put some extra thought into it. So thank you. And also thank you for inventing ice cream sandwiches. That one I had this afternoon went so good with the weather you made. I don't know how you think this stuff up. Also, thank you for my mom and dad, lightening, unicorns, television and pretty much the whole world. But outside of all that, I really need to ask you for a favor. You know about the volleyball team tryouts tomorrow? I mean, of course you know about it but . . . What I mean is, do you think you could give me a little help? I mean, with just me alone, I'm not sure I could get on the team. But I think with both of us working together, we could totally nail this. Think how awesome that would be – you and me on the volleyball team together! . . . Anyhow, just think about it. I'd really, really like to be on that team. Also, thank you for my little brother and puppies. Amen.

FRIENDSHIP

Just between us, hanging out with Jessie is the worst. I'm serious. If I want to play outside, she/he wants to play inside. If I want to go upstairs, she/he wants to go downstairs. If I say let's stay a little longer, she/he says let's leave right now. The only thing we agree on is that we don't agree on anything. Honestly, if she/he wasn't my best friend in the whole world, I probably wouldn't hang out with her/him at all.

DOING

I know people who do things. Really. Like my friend Val? She's/he's on like every sports team in the entire school. And my friend Bailey? She/He wrote an entire book of poetry. Like, for fun. She's/He's also inventing a completely new breed of turtle that no one's ever seen. Because – why wouldn't you? AND she/he bakes. So here's the thing. I have this humongous list of all these things I want to do too. But I never do them. And I figured out that if I just stopped spending like a bajillion hours a day online, I would have time to do all of them. So one day I just stopped going on Twitter and Instagram and everywhere for like three days and here's what I learned. That whole list of things that I really want to do? I don't actually want to do any of them. So yeah, all you people out there doing things, you keep on doing them. And me?

> *(Pull out phone.)*

I'll be right here on Instagram, watching you.

(Look at phone.)

Oh wow. That's a really good looking turtle.

> *(Hold up your index finger while still looking at phone.)*

Aaand "like."

> *(Tap phone. Smile.)*

Yeah.

BIRDS

It's a funny thing about memory. I can't remember my grandfather's face, but I can remember his hands. They shook all the time. And not just a little. So much, that I remember sitting next to him at breakfast and watching him holding a spoon – his hands just shaking and shaking. And me all quiet and still on the outside, but cheering so loud and so hard on the inside for the spoon to be even half full of cereal by the time it reached his mouth.

Before I was born, he used to be an artist. Not famous, but not not-famous, if you know what I mean. So one day I asked him if he would teach me to draw, and he looked at me and said, "I don't know if I can draw anymore." But I begged him and begged him til he finally took out this box of pastels and we both took one and we got some paper and he started teaching me. And his hands that maybe before had been butterflies, just trembling and fluttering all over the place, suddenly turned into birds – all still and quiet, swooping and gliding all over the paper and making the most beautiful pictures. And I said, "Grandpa, look – you can draw!" And he said, "I can't draw for me anymore, but I guess I can for you." And we spent the whole afternoon just drawing, his hands flying over the pages. And of all the pictures from that afternoon, that's the one I remember the most.

(Raise your hand, look at it, and smile.)
'Cuz that's the funny thing about memory. I can't remember my grandfather's face. But I remember his hands.

RIDICULOUS

*(NOTE: If you're a girl, Casey is a boy. If you're a
boy, Casey is a girl.)*

Everyone's always telling me how much Casey likes me. Fine.
So what. Who cares. But then they're also always saying how
everyone can tell how much I like Casey. Which is ridiculous.
And how I should, like, talk to him/her or something. Which
makes no sense at all. I mean, sure I maybe *notice* whenever
he's/she's in the same room with me. Or maybe I giggle a
little more when he's/she's around. But seriously, what does
that have to do with anything? Like he's/she's the boss of who
I notice or how much I laugh? So maybe – just maybe – I do
those things. What difference does *that* make? It doesn't mean
I *like* him/her. Seriously. Not even a little.

KNOCK, KNOCK

(Your character is going door to door, fundraising for endangered wildlife. Begin by stepping up to the imaginary door, straightening your clothes, smoothing your hair, and then knocking. Pause a moment until the person answers the door, then start.)

Hi, my name is Aubrey and I'm going door to door to spread awareness about endangered hyenas. Did you know that for just one dollar you can protect these noble creatures from being hunted to extinction? That's right, for just one dollar . . .

(React – startled – as the person you're talking to slams the door in your face.)

Whoa!

(Yelling at door.)

Well, you don't have to be rude about it!

(Turning away from the door.)

Fine. I'm sure they'll care about something besides themselves next door.

(Walk up to the next imaginary door, straighten your clothes, smooth your hair and then knock. Again, pause just a moment until the person answers the door.)

Hi, my name is Aubrey and I'm going door to door to spread awareness about endangered hyenas. Did you know that for just one dollar . . .

(React – startled and a little angry – as the person you're talking to slams the door in your face.)

Seriously!?!?

(Yelling at door.)

What is wrong with this neighborhood!

(Turning away from the door.)

Well, *everyone* on this street can't just care about themselves.

(Walk up to the next imaginary door and knock. Again, pause a moment until the person answers the door. Speak more quickly to try to get your speech in before they slam the door.)

17

Hi, my name is Aubrey and I'm going door to door to spread awareness about . . .

> *(React, as the person you're talking to slams the door in your face. Turn and talk to the whole street.)*

Alright. OK. If all you all care about is yourselves, then that's how we're gonna play this.

> *(Walk up to the next imaginary door and knock.*
> *Pause a moment until the person answers the door.)*

Hi, my name is Aubrey. Did you know that someone has been going door to door and annoying everyone about endangered hyenas? . . .

> *(Pause a moment as the person responds.)*

Yes, that's right, ma'am. Fortunately, for just one dollar, you can protect yourself from being hunted to extinction – I mean, hounded to distraction. Because for just one dollar, I will make sure that whoever is bothering everyone on the street will not come and bug you about endangered hyenas for the rest of the day . . .

> *(The person you're talking to hands you money.)*

Wow – *two* dollars! Thank you so much. Two dollars will go a long way towards protecting . . . um . . . yourself. Have a good day.

> *(Turn away from the door and look at the money in your hand.)*

Yes! OK then – don't worry endangered hyenas, I got your back.

> *(Walk up to the next imaginary door and raise your hand to knock.)*

Next!

CONTEST

(Your character is in the middle of a big game. The referee is just now asking you if you're ready.)

(Stand for a moment, lost in your own thoughts. Then suddenly look up as you hear the coach speak.)

What, coach? . . . Am I ready? Just give me one minute.

(Close your eyes for a moment as you psych yourself up to win. As you speak to yourself, pound gently on your chest.)

You can *do* this Taylor. You can *do* this Taylor! You can DO this!

(Open your eyes and stop pounding your chest. Continue speaking only to yourself, as you continue to psych yourself up.)

Keep your mind in the game, Taylor. Casey doesn't matter. Casey can never beat you. The only person you have to beat is yourself. Mind in the game. Casey doesn't exist. Only Taylor exists. You're calm. You're centered. You're in control. You've trained for this. You're in top form. You're ready.

(Close your eyes for a moment.)

You are not *playing* the game, Taylor. You *are* the game.

(Open your eyes, looking and sounding completely determined. To the coach.)

I'm ready.

(Raise your fist slightly higher than your head. Look as aggressive and focused as you can as you stare your opponent in the eyes.)

Rock. Paper. Scissors. GO!

(Shoot your hand out in the rock or paper or scissors gesture. You instantly see that you've won.)

Yeah!

ME AGAIN

I have this idea that keeps coming back – that one day I'll be walking down the street and I'll run into my future self. Me, but from twenty or fifty years from now. And I'll know it's me, because I have this scar on my arm that I got playing soccer. So I'll be walking down the street and this man/woman will just walk up to me and say, "Alex, it's me." And he'll/she'll roll up his/her sleeve and I'll see that he/she has the same scar in the same shape in the same place – and I'll know we're the same person. And he'll/she'll say, "There's so many things I want to tell you." And then he'll/she'll tell me about all the mistakes I'm going to make and how to avoid them. And about how to make sure that all the good things that are going to happen to me really do happen. And just how to make certain that my whole life turns out right. It's gonna be awesome! . . . Problem is, until that happens, I'm gonna have to keep on figuring all that stuff out for myself.

> *(Sigh. Pause a moment. Then look left and right for your future self.)*

I sure hope I get here soon. I could definitely use the help.

ARRIVAL

When he enters the room, so much earlier than expected, it's like a blast of cold air. My father. Everyone freezes. I stare at my shoes. My sister's eyes open wide. My brother picks up a book and pretends to read. We're all thinking, does he know? Can he feel that something is a little off? We look at each other, quickly, secretly, hoping he can't see our glances. Can't feel the tension. Can't hear our hearts beat. He says, in a voice that seems too loud, "And how is everyone tonight?" There is a moment of silence that lasts forever. No one wants to be the first to speak. Where is my mother? Finally, I open my mouth, uncertain what I'm about to say. And at just at that moment, like a ball of light, my mother steps through the door holding a birthday cake with all the candles lit and we jump up and yell, "Happy birthday!"

MONSTERS

Of course I know there are no monsters under the bed. Everyone knows that. But just because there never has been doesn't mean there never will be. I mean, think about it. The sun has never exploded, but one day it will. That's a fact. Or for instance, one time I got an A on a math test. *That* never happened before . . . Or after. And one time my brother actually said thank you without being asked. All kinds of things happen that never happened before. So just to be sure about the monster under the bed thing, every night when I go to bed, I always turn the lights on and off three times. To make sure they know it's me. And then I pretty much just jump from where the door is to right onto the bed. So I don't have to put my feet anywhere near – you know, *down there*. 'Cuz even though there were never monsters there before, there's a first time for everything. And anyhow, you can't be *too* careful, right?

FAR

I think for a long time you've been drifting out into a kind of invisible ocean. Drifting so far that you're almost gone. Sometimes I think I see a flag that must be flying from the very top of your mast. Or I see some light that must be from where you are, reflected on a cloud. Or I feel a breeze that I know somehow has passed by you. But it isn't you. It isn't you. And then the breeze moves on. The light goes out. The one small speck on the horizon disappears. And it's all gone. You're gone. And I'm still here.

RUDE

(Your character is at the movies, just now returning from getting popcorn in the middle of the movie. You're holding a popcorn container and aggressively squeezing along the row – disturbing everyone along the way – to get back to where your friend is sitting. Each apology is to a different person that you're squeezing by.)

'Scuse me. Pardon me. Sorry. 'Scuse me.

(The person you're trying to squeeze past doesn't move.)

I said '*scuse me . . . Excuuuse* me.

(The person lets you past. You thank him sarcastically.)

Thank you.

(As you sit down, turn to the friend you're watching the movie with. A little too loudly.)

Hey! I got popcorn. I hope you like extra butter.

(The person behind you tells you to shush. Turn around to answer.)

What! Why don't *you* shush?

(To your friend.)

Anyhow, I put a ton of butter on it.

(The person behind you tells you to be quiet again. Turn around to answer.)

Hey buddy, this is a private conversation.

(To your friend.)

Plus, I got Skittles.

(Your friend tells you to keep your voice down.)

What!? I *am* keeping my voice down. Seriously. This *is* my quiet voice. Anyhow, no one's paying attention to us. They're all too busy watching the movie. So what did I miss? . . . What do you mean you'll tell me later? What good is it gonna do me to know what I missed after the movie's over? *You're* the one who said you wanted popcorn. That's just . . .

(Your cell phone rings.)

Hold on.

(Pull out your phone, which can be real or

imaginary.)

Hello? Hey PJ.

> *(To your friend.)*

It's PJ.

> *(To PJ on the phone.)*

. . . Nothing . . . Nah, I'm just watching a movie with Morgan.

> *(The person behind you tells you to be quiet. Turn around to answer.)*

Hey, why don't *you* be quiet?

> *(To PJ on the phone.)*

What is the matter with this guy behind us anyway? Listen, I gotta hang up. Everyone at this theater is being a loser . . . Yeah, I'll call you later.

> *(Hang up. Notice your friend's seat is empty and that your friend is leaving. Calling out.)*

Hey Morgan! Morgan! Where are you going? What do you mean you can't deal with this? Deal with *what*?

> *(Louder.)*

Deal with WHAT?

> *(The person behind you tells you to be quiet. Turn around to answer.)*

No *you* be quiet!

> *(Turning back towards the movie screen. To yourself.)*

Sheesh, some people are just rude.

> *(Slouch down and eat your popcorn as you watch the movie.)*

NUMBERS

I like numbers. They're simple. Even when they're complicated they're simple. Take the number two. Two plus two equals four. It equaled four yesterday. It will equal four tomorrow. And it will always equal four. You can add it on paper or on a computer or on your fingers, and no matter what, it always equals four. But people are different. They don't add up. One day, something they say means one thing. The next day, it means the opposite. One day, having someone around adds something to your life, the next day, it takes something away. I don't get it. There are an infinite number of numbers, but if I try, I can understand them. But people – I only know a few and I can't figure them out at all.

VALENTINE
(Female Version)

Every year, it's the same thing. On Valentine's Day, I make a card. And every year since second grade, I write on it Be My Valentine and I leave it on Avery Freeman's desk. And every year he opens it up, reads what I wrote, and throws it away. I used to sign the cards, but I don't bother anymore. I just leave them on his desk, 'cuz – I don't know. And this year, same thing. I made a card. Wrote Be My Valentine. And put it on his desk in Social Studies, 'cuz that's the class where I sit right behind him. And it was like watching the same movie for the twenty-fifth time. He sat down, opened the card, read it, and then put it back in the envelope. And then he folded it in half. And then folded it in half again. And then kept on folding it until it looked like he was trying to make it so small that it would turn into nothing. With me right behind him, watching. And when he was finished folding it into this tiny little crumpled-up square of nothing, he put in the middle of his desk and just stared at the blackboard. With me right behind, just staring at him. I don't know why I even bother. It's the same thing every year. And then he turned around and I could see he had that little crumple of nothing in his hand. My crumple of nothing. And he stared at me for a second really hard, like he was mad or something. And then he said – yes.
(Starting to smile.)
He said he'd be my Valentine.
(Smiling broadly.)
This year, Avery Freeman said yes!

VALENTINE

(Male Version)

Every year, it's the same thing. On Valentine's Day, I make a card. And every year since second grade, I write on it Be My Valentine and I leave it on Avery Freeman's desk. And every year she opens it up, reads what I wrote, and throws it away. I used to sign the cards, but I don't bother anymore. I just leave them on her desk, 'cuz – I don't know. And this year, same thing. I made a card. Wrote Be My Valentine. And put it on her desk in Social Studies, 'cuz that's the class where I sit right behind her. And it was like watching the same movie for the twenty-fifth time. She sat down, opened the card, read it, and then put it back in the envelope. And then she folded it in half. And then folded it in half again. And then kept on folding it until it looked like she was trying to make it so small that it would turn into nothing. With me right behind her, watching. And when she was finished folding it into this tiny little crumpled-up square of nothing, she put in the middle of her desk and just stared at the blackboard, with me right behind, just staring at her. I don't know why I even bother. It's the same thing every year. And then she turned around and I could see she had that little crumple of nothing in her hand. My crumple of nothing. And she stared at me for a second really hard, like she was mad or something. And then she said – yes.

(Starting to smile.)

She said she'd be my Valentine.

(Smiling broadly.)

This year, Avery Freeman said yes!

VOCABULARY

Yesterday we had this vocabulary test in Mrs. Conrad's English class. Oh-my-gosh. I studied maybe a bajillion vocabulary words for, like, hours. And though I found the test to be both arduous and burdensome, I can legitimately relate that it was pedagogically edifying. I mean, seriously, like without words, how would we even talk? I feel really adamant about that. Like, if you want to pontificate, words are totally optimal . . . Or obligatory . . . One of those. Maybe both. So even though vocabulary tests are verifiably onerous, I would have to declaim that vocabulary itself is like totally, um . . . good.

ALEX

(Your character is making a phone call. Start by taking out your phone, making the call, and waiting for the other person to answer. In the pauses below, the other person is speaking. NOTE: If you're a girl, your sibling Jamie is also a girl. If you're a boy, your sibling Jamie is also a boy.)

Hi Devon?

(Enthusiastically.)

It's Alex!

(Less enthusiastically, as you realize that Devon isn't sure who you are.)

. . . Alex . . . Alex Garner. From school. We're partners in science class. And I live across the street from you . . . Yes, Jamie's brother/sister! . . . Yeah, Jamie's really cute . . . Yeah, especially in that baseball cap . . . And those shorts . . . Yeah . . . Anyway, I was calling because . . . No, he's/she's not with me, but I was thinking . . . No, he/she didn't ask me to call you, but I was wondering, umm, you know how, like, the spring dance is coming up . . . In the spring . . . Like, this spring. And I was thinking that maybe if . . .

(Devon interrupts you.)

I don't know if Jamie's going to the dance with anyone. But I was kind of wondering if . . . What? . . .

(Excitedly.)

Yeah, of course I'd do something for you! Anything! . . . What? . . . Oh . . . Yeah. Sure. I'd be really happy to ask him/her if he/ she wants to go to the dance with you . . . Yeah . . . Thanks. I think you're great too. Well, I have to go now. Yeah. Bye Devon.

(Devon calls you by the wrong name while saying goodbye.)

No – it's Alex. My name is Alex. I just . . .

(Devon hangs up. Take the phone away from your ear and look at it a moment, then put it in your pocket. To yourself.)

My name is Alex.

THE BANK

Oh, this is beautiful. So perfect. Every time me and my friends play Monopoly, I just say, "I'll be the Banker," and everyone says, "OK." It's so easy. Sooo easy. I just sit there, and maybe halfway through the game I sort of look at the ceiling and I sort of look at the floor and I sort of look around the room and then when no one's watching – boop – I just grab a few hundred dollars from the bank and bingo, I'm ahead! Of course, that doesn't mean I always win. Cuz if I, like, *borrow* too much, I might get caught and that would be bad. Plus embarrassing. But even without me winning all the time, I sometimes wonder why everyone always just trusts me to be the Banker. I mean, I wouldn't trust them. Not at all. Maybe I'm just smarter than they are . . .

(Think a moment.)

Probably . . .

(Think a moment.)

Or maybe they're all cheating, too! Those stinkers! I bet every time I look at the ceiling or look at the floor, my so-called friends are moving their pieces or maybe . . . maybe they're stealing money from *my* pile! That's why they don't care if I'm the Banker! They get me to steal the money from the bank and then *they* steal it from *me*! And that's why I don't always win! Well, I've had it. Next time, I'm not gonna ask to be Banker. I'm gonna figure out an even better way to win. I can't believe my so-called friends. Unbelievable.

(Cross your arms and glare angrily.)

Bunch of cheaters.

DARK SIDE

A few weeks ago, Mrs. Kaufman in science told us that one side of the moon always faces away from the Earth and no matter what, no one here can ever see it. Every night, one side facing away from us, forever. She called it the dark side of the moon, and except for a couple of astronauts for just a few minutes, nobody from Earth ever *has* seen it and we don't know anything about it. Now sometimes, when I'm alone in my room at night, I look up and I think about the dark side and I think there are probably gardens up there, with trees and flowers. Different from here, and more beautiful. And it's quiet there. So quiet that no matter what, you can never hear people fighting. Or crying. Or being angry. Because at like a million miles away, the only sounds that could cut through space would be happy sounds. Like my brother laughing. Or kids playing. Or my mom singing like she used to . . . I don't know. Mrs. Kaufman didn't really tell us about that part. But if it's there like I think, I'd really like to see it someday . . . Soon . . . I'd really, really like to see it.

GOALS

My father always tells me, "Sandy, it's good to have goals. First you set a goal for yourself. Then you accomplish it." And I totally agree with him. Like this morning, we had this math test in Mrs. Dugby's class. A really important math test. And I set myself the goal of not taking it. So as soon as they started passing out the test, I raised my hand and I said "Mrs. Dugby, may I be excused from the test?" And she said, "No." So I raised my hand again and I said, "Mrs. Dugby, what I meant to say was can I go to the bathroom?" And she said, "Just be quick about it. We'll wait. " Which didn't really help at all. So I raised my hand a third time and I said, "Mrs. Dugby? I mean I have to go to the bathroom because I feel sick." So she said, "Sick enough to take a make-up test tomorrow after school?" Which also was not helpful. So anyhow, this went on for probably longer than it should have. At least I'm guessing that's what Mrs. Dugby thought because now I have a new goal, which is to figure out how to not go to detention for the rest of the week. Turns out my dad was right. It's always good to have goals.

SHOP

There's a lot of things in the world, but can we get real for a minute? What's better than shopping? Seriously. There's shopping and then there's everything else. Shopping is like a universe where everything is made just for you. Anything you see, if you like it, it's yours. Well, not even yours. It's mine. Like the other day, I saw this amazing jacket, so I just said hey, I'll take it. They wrapped it up, I brought it home and it looked unbelievable. Of course, as soon as my mom saw it, she made me return it, but you know what? That's OK too. I bought it. I owned it. I wore it. And that's good enough for me. Besides, now that I got my money back, I can go shopping again tomorrow!

BIKE

There is nothing as amazing as a bicycle. With a bike, anywhere I can think of, I can go. You know – local. Or even to another town. It's like even if I don't have someone to hang out with, I still have something to do. I can just get on my bike and ride. Maybe to the park or downtown. Maybe to some street or neighborhood I've never seen before. And everywhere with new houses, and new people, and new . . . dogs. I mean, whatever! And even then, if I feel like it, I can just keep going and going until *everything* I see is new and different. And *I'm* new and different to everyone who sees *me*. I can even go so far that I see new mountains I've never seen before. And new sunsets. And new stars . . . Until I get tired and all I want is the people who already know me. And my own house. And my own dog. And then the bike turns around and it takes me back home again.

WITNESS

(Your character is being questioned about a crime he or she witnessed.)

(Place your left hand on an imaginary bible and raise your right hand, palm facing forward, to give your oath.)

I solemnly swear to tell the truth, the whole truth, and nothing but the truth.

(Take your left hand off the bible and lower your right hand.)

What I saw? I saw two men, maybe three, break in through the kitchen window. Two of the men, maybe three, had guns and all of them wore ski masks. What? Yes, I had a clear view of them. And I could hear them talking, too. The first man said, "I can't believe we're doing this." And then the second man said, "I'm really hungry." I don't remember what the third man said. Or if there was one. So the first man says, "It smells like someone's been baking cookies in here," or something like that. And then the second man says, "I sure could go for some fresh baked cookies." I'm not sure what the third man said. Or if he was even there. But then the first man says, "I think I see those cookies, right there in the corner." And then the second man says that maybe no one would even notice if just a few of the cookies were missing. And everyone thought, yeah probably not. And so they all started eating the cookies. I really think they only meant to eat just one or two, but the cookies were so good. And really chocolaty. And like, still warm from the oven. And so they just kept eating them and eating them until all the cookies were basically gone. And then they all ran away laughing. Other than that, Mom, I swear I don't know what happened to the cookies.

TIME

Time. A poem by Alex Brenner.

They say there was a big explosion the day the universe began,
I don't know,
I wasn't there,
But they say that was the beginning of time.

There was also a big explosion the day that we first met,
You should know,
You were there,
And that was the beginning
Of you being my universe.

I'll love you til the end of time,
Maybe longer,
Because real love lasts forever.

At least that's what you said.

But I guess time's a funny thing.
Because yesterday I saw you in the gym with Taylor
At 3:15
After last period.
And time stopped,
And my heart stopped,
And my universe exploded,
And I knew right there and then,
That time might have a beginning,
But it also has an end.
            (Pause a moment and look at your audience.)
This poem is definitely not dedicated to *you*, Devon. Or to
Taylor.

Thank you.

FLOWERS

OK, so this is how life is different from the movies. There's this old lady that I pass every day on the way home from school, and she's always working in her front yard planting flowers or something. And she's always alone. In the movies, one day the boy/girl would stop and ask her if she needs any help. And from there we'd slowly get to be friends and she'd learn about my dreams or whatever and I'd learn about her past and this whole thing would happen that would make us both more alive or something. So one day I'm walking by, and I say to her, "Do you need any help?" And she looks up at me and says, "Do I *look* like I need help?" Just like that. So now whenever I'm going down that block, I always walk on the other side of the street. Life is definitely not like the movies.

SNAP

It always starts with something little. Like maybe Justin, who has the desk next to mine, is snapping a rubber band. And snapping it. And snapping it. Now yeah, one part of me knows that he has no idea that he's bugging the heck out of me. On the other hand, I mean, how could he *not* know, right? It's annoying. And he's doing it over and over. So I give him a look. A really obvious look. But he pretends he doesn't see it. Or maybe he really doesn't see it. I don't care. Because now he's really bugging the heck out of me.

(Start getting a little angry.)

And it's incredibly rude. So rude that it's all I can do just to stay in my chair and not start screaming at him. So rude, that without even knowing it, I break my pencil in half and just start staring at him and staring at him. But he doesn't stop.

(Get a little angrier.)

He just keeps on snapping that rubber band and snapping it and snapping it. And I'm staring and he's snapping and he's snapping and I'm staring and I'm thinking how rude he is and why doesn't he just stop it!

(Get even angrier.)

Just stop it! JUST STOP IT! And then I stand up and . . .

(Take a few deep, angry breaths, then largely calm down.)

. . . I don't even know. I just wind up back here in the principal's office again. But how is that my fault? How is any of that my fault?

D

I got another D in Math today.

(Pull out your report card and show it to the audience. NOTE: The report card can be real or imaginary.)

Look. Here's my report card. It's right there – D. Yeah. D is the first letter of Disaster. Or Disappointed Dad. Or Don't even think about watching TV for a solid week, young man/young lady . . . Did you know that D is the fourth most common letter in the alphabet for a word to start with? It's true. Maybe you can tell, I'm really good with words. See?

(Hold up the report card again.)

I got an A in English. Right here. But I've never gotten an A in Math. Ever. I know that for a fact, cause I'm also good in History. See?

(Point to report card.)

But my Dad doesn't care about all that. He doesn't, like, subtract all the good A's from the one bad D. At least I don't think he does. You know . . .

(Pointing to self.)

. . . bad at math. But everyone can't be good at everything, right? Or then it wouldn't be called good. It would be called average. So tonight, I have to take this thing home and get my Dad to sign it. He's gonna raise seven kinds of stink about that D. But I'm not really worried, cause I know I can talk him out of the no TV thing. I always can. Cause even though I'm no good at Math, remember this A for English?

(Point to report card.)

I'm really, really good with words.

(Look at report card, smile, then put it back in your pocket.)

Game on.

EXERCISE

So I saw this show the other day that was all about building muscles or something. And basically, it was all just – do a little bit of something today and then do a little more tomorrow and, you know, more and more like that. And I started thinking. Like, maybe it can work for more than just muscles. So for instance, what if I could make myself be happy for just one minute today. And then tomorrow maybe make myself be happy for two minutes. And if I could be happy for two, then maybe the next day I could be happy for four. And on and on, just a little bit more every day, until one day I wake up and I'm just – happy. Without thinking about it. Without even trying. Just . . . happy. The way I was when you were still here.

PINCH

(Your character is at the doctor's office, about to get a shot.)

(To self, as you roll up or push up one of your sleeves as far as it will go. Nervously.)
No. No, no, no. No, no, no, no.
(Turn away from the arm with the rolled up sleeve.)
Uhhh, I hate getting shots. Just the thought of it makes me – uhh. What's the doctor doing?
(Look at the doctor, reluctantly.)
No, no, no. I can't look at this . . . He's getting out the syringe! . . . Whoa! That's a long needle. That's a really long needle. Definitely longer than average. And sharper. I can tell even from here. Now what's he doing? Argh, he's filling it up, he's filling it up! Oh no. He's coming over!
(The doctor says something. To doctor.)
What? I'll feel a little pinch? Sure. Fine.
(Looking away from the arm that's about to get the shot. To self.)
Who does he think he's fooling? A little pinch? A pinch? Since when does having someone stick a needle in your arm feel like a pinch? Compared to a needle, I would love to be pinched. I would beg to be pinched . . . Should I ask the doctor to pinch me?
(Think a moment.)
No.
(Closing your eyes.)
Ohh, this is gonna be terrible. This is gonna be . . .
(Opening eyes.)
Wait. Was that it? That barely even hurt.
(Looking at the arm where you just got the shot.)
Honestly, I really don't know why people make such a big deal out of getting a shot. Bunch of babies.
(Rubbing arm.)
I wonder if they have lollipops.

COFFEE

(Throughout the monologue, speak faster than normal, but make sure that you can still be completely understood.)

So my mom drinks coffee all the time. And I always say, can I have some, can I have some? And she always says, "You won't like it." But I figure, like really, how bad could it be if she drinks it all day every day? So every time I see her drinking coffee – which is basically every time I see her – I always say, come on, can't I just try once? I mean *every* time. Always asking her. Until finally, like an hour ago, she said, "OK, you can try a little." So she filled like maybe a quarter of a cup with this coffee and then put in a bunch of milk and a bunch of sugar, and I drank the whole thing in maybe two seconds. And it tasted really good. And I thought what is she talking about? I really like this! But then I started to feel like, I don't know, like really hyper. And I kind of wanted to calm down, but I couldn't calm down. And I started to feel more like that and more like that and more like that until – I mean, I don't even know why I'm telling you all this. I don't usually talk to pigeons. But my mom was right. I guess I really don't like coffee.

LIFE

If you think about it, TV is a lot like life. And more than that, it totally teaches us all the things we need to *know* about life. Just by being itself. So for instance, let's say there's a show you want to watch, but that show isn't on for like three whole days. TV teaches you patience. Or let's say you get like this mad crush on the star of your favorite show. TV teaches you about love. But it doesn't end there. Because you know that star will never love you back. So TV teaches you that sometimes it's OK to give love without getting it back. That's really deep. Or let's say your favorite show gets canceled. And you have no idea if you're going to see the love of your life ever, never, ever again. And let's say your sister says, "who cares, it was a lousy show anyway." And you get really mad. And you say something to her that probably you shouldn't have said. And that you definitely shouldn't have said when you realize that your mom overheard everything and she says no TV for a week. But in a way that's OK. Because after a week, TV is still there, just waiting for you. And even all the shows that you missed are right there on the TiVo box. Because TV isn't one of those things that you love, but it doesn't love you back. TV loves you back a lot. Like always. And that's good. Because if you think about it, TV is a lot like life. Or at least – it sure is a lot like my life.

RESPECT

It's been this way forever. For, like, my whole life no one has ever given me the respect that I most definitely deserve. And for the longest time I couldn't figure out why. I mean, I'm smart, I'm funny, I'm amazing at ping pong. I even smell good. Which is more than you can say about a lot of other people around here. And then it hit me. I'm not getting all the respect I deserve because I'm not tall enough. Tall people automatically get respect. I'm not kidding. You see it everywhere. A tall person walks into the room and right away everyone starts respecting them. Like subconsciously. They don't even know they're doing it. So this is my plan. At the drugstore they sell these . . . I don't know, these *things* for like twelve dollars and forty-nine cents that you put in your shoes and they instantly make you taller. And more noticed. And getting the exact amount of respect that you always deserved. And I'm totally ready for that. Now all I have to do is figure out how to get the twelve dollars and forty-nine cents.

(*Think a moment, then look to the side and call out.*)

MOM!

(*Exit in the direction you looked.*)

JUMP

(Your character standing is on top of a very high rock, considering jumping into the water below. Several friends are down in the water, watching.)

(To self. Looking down at the water.)
Whoa. This rock is a lot higher than it looked from down there. And the water looks a lot harder.
(Out loud to friends below. Loudly.)
Yeah, of course I'm gonna jump. Why wouldn't I jump?
(To self.)
OK, get it together. You're the last one and they're all looking.
(Out loud to friends below.)
What are you even talking about? Of course I'm not scared. Why would I be scared? I'm just thinking about if I should do a backflip or not.
(To self.)
Ugh. What was I even thinking? Why did I tell everyone I would jump off this dumb rock anyway?
(Out loud.)
No, Devon, *you're* the coward. I'm just trying to build up some suspense. Seriously. I'm practically bored already.
(To self.)
Don't think, just do it. Don't think, just do it. Don't think, just do it.
(Out loud.)
OK, ready? I don't want anyone to miss it. It would be *super* boring to have to do it again.
(To self.)
Never again. Never again. I am never, ever doing this again. Ready, and . . .
(Close your eyes tightly, take a step or two and - with eyes still tightly closed - jump off the rock. Scream.)
Aghhhhhhh.
(As you scream and "fall," slowly lower yourself to a crouching position. After you've landed in the water, stay squatting for an extra moment or two,

then open your eyes. Cautiously look left, then right.
To self.)

Phew!

(Raise both arms in victory. Out loud.)

Ta da!

HAPPY

(Throughout the following phone call, no matter how many times you tell the person on the other end how happy you are, your face, body language and every gesture continually show how very not happy you really are.)

Hello? . . . Oh hey . . . What? Yeah. Of course I'm happy you called . . . Yeah. Really happy . . . Oh, was it tonight we said I was going to help you with your math homework instead of watching TV? . . . What? . . . No, yeah, of course I remember. We totally said it was tonight. Yeah. That I was gonna come all the way over to your house and help you with your homework because you're allergic to my cat and so you can't come over here . . . Yeah . . . And I'm totally happy to do it because my mom told your mom that I would be totally happy to do it. And if both our mom's are happy, then I'm happy, too. And not grounded. So – eight o'clock? Great. So happy you called. Happy, happy.

(Hang up and look at the phone, not happy at all.)

TREE

(Your character is standing in a park.)

You see that tree? Before my grandma moved to Florida, we used to come to this park together sometimes. And every time she would tell me how when she was my age she used to climb that tree every day. And how every day she'd go a little bit higher and a little bit higher, until she could finally get all the way to the top. My mom doesn't like that story and tells me that tree is too dangerous to climb. But sometimes, I have this dream where I'm here in the park, and I start climbing the tree, going higher and higher. And somehow, way up in the middle, I run into my grandma. Only she's my age. And she's climbing too. And right away, we recognize each other and she says, "Come on. Let's go all the way to the top." And so we climb and climb until we're finally so high up that we can see the entire world. And right then, she turns to me and says, "This is it. This is what I wanted you to see." And we just sit there, looking out at the whole world until the sun begins to go down and my grandma says, "It's getting late. Time to go back to where we started." And then she smiles at me and we climb back down.

QUITO

(Your character is taking a test. You're speaking to the person at the next desk, trying not to be heard by the teacher. The pauses in the monologue are when another person is speaking. NOTE: The city towards the end of the monologue is pronounced KEE-toe.)

Psst – what's the answer to number three? . . . No, number three – the capital of Ecuador. Is it Ecuador City? . . . No, I know Ecuador is a country, but is the capital called Ecuador City? Cuz that would make sense, right? . . . Why is that a dopey question? I mean, the capital of China wouldn't be wouldn't be called Ecuador City, right? It would be called, like, China City or something – I don't know. Can you just tell me? . . . Fine. Then don't, but . . .

> *(Looking up suddenly and speaking, more loudly, to the teacher.)*

What's that Mrs. Grundel? No I just have, um, something stuck in my throat . . . Then I should bring my throat over to that desk in the corner? Fine.

> *(Standing up and picking up your test while speaking more quietly again to your friend at the next desk.)*

I can't believe you wouldn't – oh wait, I remember! The capital of Ecuador is Quito!

> *(Looking up suddenly and speaking again to the teacher.)*

I'm moving. I'm moving.

> *(Starting to walk off. Happily, to yourself.)*

Oh yeah, I got this.

FLIGHT

(Your character is on a long plane ride. Sit slumped in a chair, looking bored and uncomfortable. Take a few moments before you start to talk. Change your position. Look around. Look annoyed, then bored again. Etc.)

Oh. My. Gosh. Oh my gosh. Ohhh my gosh. Why do plane rides have to take so long? I feel like I've been sitting here forever. Plus a month. And then another week. It's like the plane ride that never ended. Maybe two years from now, this plane will land somewhere and they'll look in the back and see that all the passengers have died of boredom. Seriously. There's nothing to do but sit here. And maybe eat some chips. Or watch movies on this tiny screen. Or play video games. Or sleep. But if I was home right now, I could totally be . . . well . . . eating chips or . . . watching movies or . . . playing video games . . . Hunh.

(Change to more "up" mood as you realize what you've just said.)

Well, alright then. Note to self: Maybe plane rides aren't so bad.

(Calling out to the flight attendant.)

Excuse me! Can I get some more chips!

(Lean in to look at the screen in front of you.)

Now let's see what movies they got.

PAIN

Last week I saw this show on TV where they were talking about if plants can feel pain or whatever. And there were a bunch of people who basically said no, plants can't possibly feel pain because they have no brains. Or nerves. Or pretty much anything else you would need. And that kind of made sense. But then there were like these other people that said nuh uh. Just because you can't figure out *how* a plant could feel pain that doesn't mean that it *doesn't*. And I thought, yeah, I bet plants *do* feel pain. Or at least that's what I told my dad right after he asked me to mow the lawn. But then my dad said, do you think it would cause the grass more pain than, for instance, a spanking? So I guess he won that time. But just wait til he hears my reason for not having to take out the garbage. Un. Beatable.

LIFESAVER

I saved a life this morning. Seriously. I was just walking along past this ginormous puddle, when I looked down and I saw this yellow jacket or bumblebee just flopping around in the water. Like in a really desperate way. And I could tell he couldn't get out. And that if I just left him there, he would totally drown. So even though I really hate getting stung by bees or yellow jackets or whatever, I just instantly bent down and scooped him up and put him on the ground. And he immediately went from desperate, "I don't want to die," flopping around to, like, a bug with a mission. He literally spent the next 10 minutes like whizzing his wings at about a million times a second to dry them off, and like grooming his fur, or whatever it is that bees or yellow jackets have. And wiping off tiny drops of water from his legs. You just knew that he was happy to be out of the water and that all he wanted was to get back in the game. And then – he just flew off. And I thought, "I did that." I saved his life. And I know you're probably thinking, well yeah, but it was a really small life. But here's the thing – to that bee, it wasn't a small life at all. It was everything. His little life was as important to him as my big life is to me. And now I feel kind of like I'm never going to be scared of getting stung again. Because I saved his life. And now I'm like a friend to the bees. Or maybe the yellow jackets. Whatever.

PROCRASTINATION

My mom is always complaining about how much I like to procrastinate and I'm always like, can't we talk about this later? I mean, sure, I like to procrastinate. But if I didn't put off doing stuff until tomorrow, then I might not have anything to *do* tomorrow. Which would be terrible. And, I mean, isn't tomorrow basically just today, but later? And yeah, of course I sometimes think that maybe I should figure out a way to like, stop putting things off so much. But seriously, that's not something I need to think about right now, is it?

POINTLESS

(Your character is lying in bed. To self.)

What am I doing? What am I doing? What am I doing? I should get out of bed. Right now . . .
(Lie silently for a moment. Don't even make an attempt to sit up.)
But what's the point? Even if I got out of bed, what would I do then? No one calls. For all my so-called friends care, I could stay in bed all day. I could stay in bed til the sun explodes. I bet they wouldn't even notice . . .
(Lie silently for a moment.)
I should probably at least take a shower . . . But why bother? No one's gonna smell me.
(Smell your armpit.)
Anyhow, I'm fine. What if I never got out of bed? What if I just stayed here forever until one day one of my so-called friends actually thought about me for two seconds and they came up and found me covered with dust. Or mold. Or mice. Yeah – probably mice. Then they'd feel pretty ridiculous, like "Oh, I guess we should have called before the mice got him/her." Or maybe even –
(Your phone rings, breaking your train of thought.)
Whoa! Phone.
(You start to frantically look for the phone, which you know is somewhere on the bed or under the covers.)
Phone, phone, phone.
(You find the phone.)
There you are!
(Answering phone.)
Hello? . . . Jessie? . . . Nothing. Just – planning my day . . . You mean now? With everybody? Um, yeah, I guess I could fit you guys in . . . Yeah – twenty minutes? Perfect.
(Hang up the phone. To self.)
Sheesh. And just when I was planning on having a relaxing day at home.
(Shrug. Then smile.)

ALBUM

(Your character is showing photos on a cell phone, scrolling through one at a time. The phone can be real or imaginary. NOTE: If you're a boy, Bailey is a girl and Jordan is a boy. If you're a girl, Bailey is a boy and Jordan is a girl.)

(Look at your phone, select the photo, then hold the phone up for the audience to see.)

So this is the first one. I don't know if you can see this, but that's Bailey at a gymnastics competition I went to with some friends before I really knew him/her.

(Scroll to next photo, then hold phone up for the audience.)

This is all of us eating burgers after the gymnastics competition. That's Bailey at the end of the table.

(Scroll to next photo, then hold phone up for the audience.)

This is me and Bailey in the park, like a week later. He's/She's doing a handstand and wearing that sweatshirt that he/she always wears.

(Scroll to next photo, then hold phone up for the audience.)

And this is a picture somebody took at lunch of me and Bailey with straws up our noses.

(Glance at the photo.)

Funny.

(Scroll to next photo, then hold phone up for the audience.)

Oh – here we are at Bailey's birthday party that time he/she went to blow out the candles and wound up spitting all over the cake. He's/She's got on that new sweatshirt I gave him/her for a present.

(Scroll to next photo, then hold phone up for the audience.)

This one's of us pretending to do homework in study hall, but, you know, not.

*(Scroll to next photo, then hold phone up for the
audience.)*

And here's Bailey with this girl/boy Jordan in a picture I took
when they didn't know I was like ten feet away. They're in the
park and Bailey has his/her hand on Jordan's shoulder and
they're laughing. If you zoom in, you can see that Bailey's not
wearing the sweatshirt I gave him/her.

*(Stare at the photo angrily for a moment. Scroll to
the next photo and hold phone up for the audience.)*

This is the video I sent Bailey after I saw him/her and Jordan
in the park. I'm like *really* telling him/her what I think of
him/her.

*(Scroll to next photo, then hold phone up for the
audience.)*

And this is a selfie I took of me alone in the park after I sent
the video and we had that big fight and he/she said he/she
never wanted to see me again. Well guess what. I never want
to see you again either.

(Hold index finger over phone.)

Delete album.

*(Tap delete button on your phone. Hold up phone
again.)*

You're gone.

WEEKEND

So last month, my family took a vacation to this place so far away from anywhere you'd want to be that there isn't even any cell phone service. I'm not kidding. And my mom said, Oh Taylor, stop worrying. It'll be amazing. We'll all get to spend some real time together and you'll get to see what things were like when I grew up, before there even *were* cell phones. And I have to tell you, my mom was right. It really *was* amazing. We all spent lots of time together, and we played board games, and I went on these long walks with my dad, and I wasn't constantly getting like a million messages a day. Before that vacation, I never really understood how *calm* the world used to be. Honestly, it was probably the worst weekend of my life.

GOOD-BYE

(In the following monologue, your friend Devon can be a boy or a girl – whatever feels right for you.)

In this play we're doing, there's a scene at the end of the first act where my character tells Devon's character what a good friend he/she always was and how much I'm gonna miss him/her. And it got me thinking about when me and Devon really *did* used to be friends and all the stuff we used to do together. I mean, the first play I ever tried out for, me and Devon auditioned for it together. Practically every afternoon we used to be at each other's houses. And I keep thinking how funny it is that we don't even talk to each other now except when we're on stage. And I just wonder if when we're rehearsing that good-bye scene and I'm standing there and saying these things about what a good friend he/she was, and how much I'm gonna miss him/her – I wonder if he/she can see where the acting ends and where I begin. I mean . . . I wonder if he/she can see that I really don't want to say good-bye at all.

NOTES

NOTES

NOTES

DOUGLAS M. PARKER is an award-winning playwright and lyricist, as well as the author of the best-selling books *Contemporary Monologues for Young Actors*, *Fantasy Monologues for Young Actors* and *Contemporary Scenes for Young Actors*. His theatrical works include the musical, *Life on the Mississippi* (book and lyrics), based on Mark Twain's classic autobiographical coming-of-age tale; *BESSIE: The Life and Music of Bessie Smith*, based on the rise and fall of the great American blues singer; *Thicker Than Water*, a drama based on the Andrea Yates tragedy; *Declarations*, a Young Audience historical drama drawn from the letters of John and Abigail Adams from their earliest courtship through the summer of 1776; and *The Private History of a Campaign That Failed*, a Young Audience comedy based on Mark Twain's true, humorous memoir of his time as a lieutenant in the Confederacy's least accomplished, most forgotten regiment. He can be reached at MonologueFrog@gmail.com.

www.ingramcontent.com/pod-product-compliance
Lightning Source LLC
Chambersburg PA
CBHW070025110426
42741CB00034B/2563